Sewing Journal
For all your sewing projects

Sewing Journal

This handy Journal will help you keep track of your sewing project in one handy book. You can reflect back on past creations and check all the points that were important, helping you keep track of elements of a project that worked well or needed development.

How to use this Journal

Section 1

- Keep track of all your sewing projects in the 'Index of patterns'.
- Place all important measurements for Individuals in the 'Measurements' section for future reference.
- Use the "Notes' section for any other important information you need to keep at hand.

Section 2

With spaces for 54 patterns in total, each double page spread consists of space for:

- Pattern Information
- Fabric Swatches
- Fabric specification – Trims; Colour; Width; length; Supplier; Cost
- Front and back working drawings / sketches
- Alternations needed
- Machine settings
- Photograph of final product
- Evaluation
- Additional notes

Index of patterns

Pattern name	Client	Completed

Pattern name	Client	Completed

Pattern name	Client	Completed

Measurements

Name			
Bust		Neck	
Waist		Nape to waist	
Hip		Waist to hip	
Chest		Wait to floor	
Shoulder		Inside leg	

Name			
Bust		Neck	
Waist		Nape to waist	
Hip		Waist to hip	
Chest		Wait to floor	
Shoulder		Inside leg	

Name			
Bust		Neck	
Waist		Nape to waist	
Hip		Waist to hip	
Chest		Wait to floor	
Shoulder		Inside leg	

Name			
Bust		Neck	
Waist		Nape to waist	
Hip		Waist to hip	
Chest		Wait to floor	
Shoulder		Inside leg	

Measurements

Name			
Bust		Neck	
Waist		Nape to waist	
Hip		Waist to hip	
Chest		Wait to floor	
Shoulder		Inside leg	

Name			
Bust		Neck	
Waist		Nape to waist	
Hip		Waist to hip	
Chest		Wait to floor	
Shoulder		Inside leg	

Name			
Bust		Neck	
Waist		Nape to waist	
Hip		Waist to hip	
Chest		Wait to floor	
Shoulder		Inside leg	

Name			
Bust		Neck	
Waist		Nape to waist	
Hip		Waist to hip	
Chest		Wait to floor	
Shoulder		Inside leg	

Measurements

Name			
Bust		Neck	
Waist		Nape to waist	
Hip		Waist to hip	
Chest		Wait to floor	
Shoulder		Inside leg	

Name			
Bust		Neck	
Waist		Nape to waist	
Hip		Waist to hip	
Chest		Wait to floor	
Shoulder		Inside leg	

Name			
Bust		Neck	
Waist		Nape to waist	
Hip		Waist to hip	
Chest		Wait to floor	
Shoulder		Inside leg	

Name			
Bust		Neck	
Waist		Nape to waist	
Hip		Waist to hip	
Chest		Wait to floor	
Shoulder		Inside leg	

Notes:

Notes:

Notes:

Pattern

The pattern:

_____

_____

_____

_____

_____

Fabric swatches

Fabric / Trims	Colour	Width	Length	Supplier	Cost

Working drawing – Front

Working drawing – Back

Alterations needed:
_____
_____
_____

Machine settings:
_____
_____

Photograph of final item

Evaluation:
_____
_____
_____
_____
_____

Additional notes

Pattern

The pattern:

_____

_____

_____

_____

_____

_____

Fabric swatches

Fabric / Trims	Colour	Width	Length	Supplier	Cost

Working drawing - Front

Working drawing - Back

Alterations needed:

_____
_____
_____

Machine settings:

_____
_____

Photograph of final item

Evaluation:

_____
_____
_____
_____
_____

Additional notes

Pattern

The pattern:
_____
_____
_____
_____
_____

Fabric swatches

Fabric / Trims	Colour	Width	Length	Supplier	Cost

Working drawing – Front

Working drawing – Back

Alterations needed:
_____
_____
_____

Machine settings:
_____
_____

Photograph of final item

Evaluation:
_____
_____
_____
_____
_____

Additional notes

Pattern

The pattern:

_ _

_ _

_ _

_ _

_ _

_ _

Fabric swatches

Fabric / Trims	Colour	Width	Length	Supplier	Cost

Working drawing – Front

Working drawing – Back

Alterations needed:

_____

_____

_____

Machine settings:

_____

_____

Photograph of final item

Evaluation:

_____

_____

_____

_____

_____

Additional notes

Pattern

The pattern:

_____

_____

_____

_____

_____

Fabric swatches

Fabric / Trims	Colour	Width	Length	Supplier	Cost

Working drawing – Front

Working drawing – Back

Alterations needed:
_____
_____
_____

Machine settings:
_____
_____

Photograph of final item

Evaluation:
_____
_____
_____
_____
_____

Additional notes

Pattern

The pattern:

_____

_____

_____

_____

_____

_____

Fabric swatches

Fabric / Trims	Colour	Width	Length	Supplier	Cost

Working drawing - Front

Working drawing - Back

Alterations needed:
_____
_____
_____

Machine settings:
_____
_____

Photograph of final item

Evaluation:
_____
_____
_____
_____
_____

Additional notes

Pattern

The pattern:

Fabric swatches

Fabric / Trims	Colour	Width	Length	Supplier	Cost

Working drawing – Front

Working drawing – Back

Alterations needed:

Machine settings:

Photograph of final item

Evaluation:

Additional notes

Pattern

The pattern:

_____

_____

_____

_____

_____

_____

Fabric swatches

Fabric / Trims	Colour	Width	Length	Supplier	Cost

Working drawing – Front

Working drawing – Back

Alterations needed:
_____
_____
_____

Machine settings:
_____
_____

Photograph of final item

Evaluation:
_____
_____
_____
_____
_____

Additional notes

Pattern

The pattern:
_____
_____
_____
_____
_____

Fabric swatches

Fabric / Trims	Colour	Width	Length	Supplier	Cost

Working drawing – Front

Working drawing – Back

Alterations needed:
_____
_____
_____

Machine settings:
_____
_____

Photograph of final item

Evaluation:
_____
_____
_____
_____
_____

Additional notes

Pattern

The pattern:

Fabric swatches

Fabric / Trims	Colour	Width	Length	Supplier	Cost

Working drawing – Front

Working drawing – Back

Alterations needed:
_____
_____
_____

Machine settings:
_____
_____

Photograph of final item

Evaluation:
_____
_____
_____
_____
_____

Additional notes

Pattern

The pattern:

_____

_____

_____

_____

_____

Fabric swatches

Fabric / Trims	Colour	Width	Length	Supplier	Cost

Working drawing – Front

Working drawing – Back

Alterations needed:
_____
_____
_____

Machine settings:
_____
_____

Photograph of final item

Evaluation:
_____
_____
_____
_____
_____

Additional notes

Pattern

The pattern:

_____

_____

_____

_____

_____

Fabric swatches

Fabric / Trims	Colour	Width	Length	Supplier	Cost

Working drawing - Front

Working drawing - Back

Alterations needed:
_____
_____
_____

Machine settings:
_____
_____

Photograph of final item

Evaluation:
_____
_____
_____
_____
_____

Additional notes

Pattern

The pattern:

_____

_____

_____

_____

_____

Fabric swatches

Fabric / Trims	Colour	Width	Length	Supplier	Cost

Working drawing – Front

Working drawing – Back

Alterations needed:

_____
_____
_____

Machine settings:

_____
_____

Photograph of final item

Evaluation:

_____
_____
_____
_____
_____

Additional notes

Pattern

The pattern:

_ _

_ _

_ _

_ _

_ _

_ _

Fabric swatches

Fabric / Trims	Colour	Width	Length	Supplier	Cost

Working drawing – Front

Working drawing – Back

Alterations needed:

_____

_____

_____

Machine settings:

_____

_____

Photograph of final item

Evaluation:

_____

_____

_____

_____

_____

Additional notes

Pattern

The pattern:

_____

_____

_____

_____

_____

Fabric swatches

Fabric / Trims	Colour	Width	Length	Supplier	Cost

Working drawing – Front

Working drawing – Back

Alterations needed:
_____
_____
_____

Machine settings:
_____
_____

Photograph of final item

Evaluation:
_____
_____
_____
_____
_____

Additional notes

Pattern

The pattern:

_____

_____

_____

_____

_____

_____

Fabric swatches

Fabric / Trims	Colour	Width	Length	Supplier	Cost

Working drawing – Front

Working drawing – Back

Alterations needed:
_____
_____
_____

Machine settings:
_____
_____

Photograph of final item

Evaluation:
_____
_____
_____
_____
_____

Additional notes

Pattern

The pattern:

Fabric swatches

Fabric / Trims	Colour	Width	Length	Supplier	Cost

Working drawing – Front

Working drawing – Back

Alterations needed:
_____
_____
_____

Machine settings:
_____
_____

Photograph of final item

Evaluation:
_____
_____
_____
_____
_____

Additional notes

Pattern

The pattern:

_____

_____

_____

_____

_____

Fabric swatches

Fabric / Trims	Colour	Width	Length	Supplier	Cost

Working drawing – Front

Working drawing – Back

Alterations needed:
_____
_____
_____

Machine settings:
_____
_____

Photograph of final item

Evaluation:
_____
_____
_____
_____
_____

Additional notes

Pattern

The pattern:

_____

_____

_____

_____

_____

Fabric swatches

Fabric / Trims	Colour	Width	Length	Supplier	Cost

Working drawing – Front

Working drawing – Back

Alterations needed:

Machine settings:

Photograph of final item

Evaluation:

Additional notes

Pattern

The pattern:

_____

_____

_____

_____

_____

_____

Fabric swatches

Fabric / Trims	Colour	Width	Length	Supplier	Cost

Working drawing – Front

Working drawing – Back

Alterations needed:
_____
_____
_____

Machine settings:
_____
_____

Photograph of final item

Evaluation:
_____
_____
_____
_____
_____

Additional notes

Pattern

The pattern:

Fabric swatches

Fabric / Trims	Colour	Width	Length	Supplier	Cost

Working drawing – Front

Working drawing – Back

Alterations needed:
_____
_____
_____

Machine settings:
_____
_____

Photograph of final item

Evaluation:
_____
_____
_____
_____
_____

Additional notes

Pattern

The pattern:

_____

_____

_____

_____

_____

Fabric swatches

Fabric / Trims	Colour	Width	Length	Supplier	Cost

Working drawing – Front

Working drawing – Back

Alterations needed:

_____

_____

_____

Machine settings:

_____

_____

Photograph of final item

Evaluation:

_____

_____

_____

_____

_____

Additional notes

Pattern

The pattern:

_____

_____

_____

_____

_____

Fabric swatches

Fabric / Trims	Colour	Width	Length	Supplier	Cost

Working drawing – Front

Working drawing – Back

Alterations needed:

Machine settings:

Photograph of final item

Evaluation:

Additional notes

Pattern

The pattern:

_____

_____

_____

_____

_____

_____

Fabric swatches

Fabric / Trims	Colour	Width	Length	Supplier	Cost

Working drawing – Front

Working drawing – Back

Alterations needed:

_____

_____

_____

Machine settings:

_____

_____

Photograph of final item

Evaluation:

_____

_____

_____

_____

_____

Additional notes

Pattern

The pattern:

Fabric swatches

Fabric / Trims	Colour	Width	Length	Supplier	Cost

Working drawing – Front

Working drawing – Back

Alterations needed:
_____
_____
_____

Machine settings:
_____
_____

Photograph of final item

Evaluation:
_____
_____
_____
_____
_____

Additional notes

Pattern

The pattern:

_____

_____

_____

_____

_____

_____

Fabric swatches

Fabric / Trims	Colour	Width	Length	Supplier	Cost

Working drawing – Front

Working drawing – Back

Alterations needed:

_____

_____

_____

Machine settings:

_____

_____

Photograph of final item

Evaluation:

_____

_____

_____

_____

_____

Additional notes

Pattern

The pattern:

_____

_____

_____

_____

_____

_____

Fabric swatches

Fabric / Trims	Colour	Width	Length	Supplier	Cost

Working drawing – Front

Working drawing – Back

Alterations needed:

_____

_____

_____

Machine settings:

_____

_____

Photograph of final item

Evaluation:

_____

_____

_____

_____

_____

Additional notes

Pattern

The pattern:

_____

_____

_____

_____

_____

Fabric swatches

Fabric / Trims	Colour	Width	Length	Supplier	Cost

Working drawing – Front

Working drawing – Back

Alterations needed:
_____
_____
_____

Machine settings:
_____
_____

Photograph of final item

Evaluation:
_____
_____
_____
_____
_____

Additional notes

Pattern

The pattern:

_____

_____

_____

_____

_____

_____

Fabric swatches

Fabric / Trims	Colour	Width	Length	Supplier	Cost

Working drawing – Front

Working drawing – Back

Alterations needed:
_____
_____
_____

Machine settings:
_____
_____

Photograph of final item

Evaluation:
_____
_____
_____
_____
_____

Additional notes

Pattern

The pattern:

_____

_____

_____

_____

_____

_____

Fabric swatches

Fabric / Trims	Colour	Width	Length	Supplier	Cost

Working drawing – Front

Working drawing – Back

Alterations needed:

_____

_____

_____

Machine settings:

_____

_____

Photograph of final item

Evaluation:

_____

_____

_____

_____

Additional notes

Pattern

The pattern:

_____

_____

_____

_____

_____

Fabric swatches

Fabric / Trims	Colour	Width	Length	Supplier	Cost

Working drawing – Front

Working drawing – Back

Alterations needed:
_____
_____
_____

Machine settings:
_____
_____

Photograph of final item

Evaluation:
_____
_____
_____
_____
_____

Additional notes

Pattern

The pattern:

_____

_____

_____

_____

_____

_____

Fabric swatches

Fabric / Trims	Colour	Width	Length	Supplier	Cost

Working drawing – Front

Working drawing – Back

Alterations needed:
_____
_____
_____

Machine settings:
_____
_____

Photograph of final item

Evaluation:
_____
_____
_____
_____
_____

Additional notes

Pattern

The pattern:
_____

_____

_____

_____

_____

_____

Fabric swatches

Fabric / Trims	Colour	Width	Length	Supplier	Cost

Working drawing – Front

Working drawing – Back

Alterations needed:

Machine settings:

Photograph of final item

Evaluation:

Additional notes

Pattern

The pattern:

Fabric swatches

Fabric / Trims	Colour	Width	Length	Supplier	Cost

Working drawing – Front

Working drawing – Back

Alterations needed:
_____
_____
_____

Machine settings:
_____
_____

Photograph of final item

Evaluation:
_____
_____
_____
_____
_____

Additional notes

Pattern

The pattern:

_____

_____

_____

_____

_____

Fabric swatches

Fabric / Trims	Colour	Width	Length	Supplier	Cost

Working drawing - Front

Working drawing - Back

Alterations needed:
_____
_____
_____

Machine settings:
_____
_____

Photograph of final item

Evaluation:
_____
_____
_____
_____
_____

Additional notes

Pattern

The pattern:

Fabric swatches

Fabric / Trims	Colour	Width	Length	Supplier	Cost

Working drawing – Front

Working drawing – Back

Alterations needed:
_____
_____
_____

Machine settings:
_____
_____

Photograph of final item

Evaluation:
_____
_____
_____
_____
_____

Additional notes

Pattern

The pattern:

_____

_____

_____

_____

_____

_____

Fabric swatches

Fabric / Trims	Colour	Width	Length	Supplier	Cost

Working drawing – Front

Working drawing – Back

Alterations needed:
_____
_____
_____

Machine settings:
_____
_____

Photograph of final item

Evaluation:
_____
_____
_____
_____
_____

Additional notes

Pattern

The pattern:

_____

_____

_____

_____

_____

Fabric swatches

Fabric / Trims	Colour	Width	Length	Supplier	Cost

Working drawing – Front

Working drawing – Back

Alterations needed:

―――――――――――――――――――――――――――
―――――――――――――――――――――――――――
―――――――――――――――――――――――――――

Machine settings:

―――――――――――――――――――――――――
―――――――――――――――――――――――――

Photograph of final item

Evaluation:

―――――――――――――――――――――――――
―――――――――――――――――――――――――
―――――――――――――――――――――――――
―――――――――――――――――――――――――
―――――――――――――――――――――――――

Additional notes

Pattern

The pattern:

_____

_____

_____

_____

_____

Fabric swatches

Fabric / Trims	Colour	Width	Length	Supplier	Cost

Working drawing – Front

Working drawing – Back

Alterations needed:
_____
_____
_____

Machine settings:
_____
_____

Photograph of final item

Evaluation:
_____
_____
_____
_____
_____

Additional notes

Pattern

The pattern:

_____

_____

_____

_____

_____

_____

Fabric swatches

Fabric / Trims	Colour	Width	Length	Supplier	Cost

Working drawing – Front

Working drawing – Back

Alterations needed:
_____
_____
_____

Machine settings:
_____
_____

Photograph of final item

Evaluation:
_____
_____
_____
_____
_____

Additional notes

Pattern

The pattern:

Fabric swatches

Fabric / Trims	Colour	Width	Length	Supplier	Cost

Working drawing – Front

Working drawing – Back

Alterations needed:
_____
_____
_____

Machine settings:
_____
_____

Photograph of final item

Evaluation:
_____
_____
_____
_____
_____

Additional notes

Pattern

The pattern:

―――――――――――――――――――

―――――――――――――――――――

―――――――――――――――――――

―――――――――――――――――――

―――――――――――――――――――

Fabric swatches

Fabric / Trims	Colour	Width	Length	Supplier	Cost

Working drawing – Front

Working drawing – Back

Alterations needed:

Machine settings:

Photograph of final item

Evaluation:

Additional notes

Pattern

The pattern:
_____

_____

_____

_____

_____

Fabric swatches

Fabric / Trims	Colour	Width	Length	Supplier	Cost

Working drawing – Front

Working drawing – Back

Alterations needed:

_____

_____

_____

Machine settings:

_____

_____

Photograph of final item

Evaluation:

_____

_____

_____

_____

_____

Additional notes

Pattern

The pattern:

_____

_____

_____

_____

_____

Fabric swatches

Fabric / Trims	Colour	Width	Length	Supplier	Cost

Working drawing – Front

Working drawing – Back

Alterations needed:
_____
_____
_____

Machine settings:
_____
_____

Photograph of final item

Evaluation:
_____
_____
_____
_____
_____

Additional notes

Pattern

The pattern:

_____

_____

_____

_____

_____

Fabric swatches

Fabric / Trims	Colour	Width	Length	Supplier	Cost

Working drawing - Front

Working drawing - Back

Alterations needed:
_____
_____
_____

Machine settings:
_____
_____

Photograph of final item

Evaluation:
_____
_____
_____
_____
_____

Additional notes

Pattern

The pattern:

_____

_____

_____

_____

_____

_____

Fabric swatches

Fabric / Trims	Colour	Width	Length	Supplier	Cost

Working drawing – Front

Working drawing – Back

Alterations needed:
_____
_____
_____

Machine settings:
_____
_____

Photograph of final item

Evaluation:
_____
_____
_____
_____
_____

Additional notes

Pattern

The pattern:

Fabric swatches

Fabric / Trims	Colour	Width	Length	Supplier	Cost

Working drawing – Front

Working drawing – Back

Alterations needed:

_____

_____

_____

Machine settings:

_____

_____

Photograph of final item

Evaluation:

_____

_____

_____

_____

_____

Additional notes

Pattern

The pattern:

Fabric swatches

Fabric / Trims	Colour	Width	Length	Supplier	Cost

Working drawing – Front

Working drawing – Back

Alterations needed:
_____
_____
_____

Machine settings:
_____
_____

Photograph of final item

Evaluation:
_____
_____
_____
_____
_____

Additional notes

Pattern

The pattern:

Fabric swatches

Fabric / Trims	Colour	Width	Length	Supplier	Cost

Working drawing – Front

Working drawing – Back

Alterations needed:
_____
_____
_____

Machine settings:
_____
_____

Photograph of final item

Evaluation:
_____
_____
_____
_____
_____

Additional notes

Pattern

The pattern:

Fabric swatches

Fabric / Trims	Colour	Width	Length	Supplier	Cost

Working drawing – Front

Working drawing – Back

Alterations needed:

_____

_____

_____

Machine settings:

_____

_____

Photograph of final item

Evaluation:

_____

_____

_____

_____

_____

Additional notes

Pattern

The pattern:

Fabric swatches

Fabric / Trims	Colour	Width	Length	Supplier	Cost

Working drawing – Front

Working drawing – Back

Alterations needed:
_____
_____
_____

Machine settings:
_____
_____

Photograph of final item

Evaluation:
_____
_____
_____
_____
_____

Additional notes

Pattern

The pattern:

Fabric swatches

Fabric / Trims	Colour	Width	Length	Supplier	Cost

Working drawing – Front

Working drawing – Back

Alterations needed:
_____
_____
_____

Machine settings:
_____
_____

Photograph of final item

Evaluation:
_____
_____
_____
_____
_____

Additional notes

Pattern

The pattern:

Fabric swatches

Fabric / Trims	Colour	Width	Length	Supplier	Cost

Working drawing – Front

Working drawing – Back

Alterations needed:

_____

_____

_____

Machine settings:

_____

_____

Photograph of final item

Evaluation:

_____

_____

_____

_____

_____

Additional notes

Pattern

The pattern:

Fabric swatches

Fabric / Trims	Colour	Width	Length	Supplier	Cost

Working drawing – Front

Working drawing – Back

Alterations needed:
_____
_____
_____

Machine settings:
_____
_____

Photograph of final item

Evaluation:
_____
_____
_____
_____
_____

Additional notes

Notes:

Notes:

Notes:

All work is copyright
© Thread and Paper Journals
2018

Made in the USA
Las Vegas, NV
22 May 2021